Before You Begin

A Message from the Woman I Am Now Th[illegible] reckoning. A rebirth. Every page you're about to read was written with raw hands and an open heart. These words were born through pain, but they don't live there anymore. They live in power now. This is your invitation to meet yourself inside every chapter.

Inside these 20 chapters, I don't just tell you what happened to me — I tell you how I found my way back. Not all at once. Not in a straight line. But piece by piece, after burying the version of myself that kept me bound to cycles I had outgrown. You're going to feel something in these pages. It may be grief. It may be anger. Maybe the softness you've had to hide for too long. But you'll also feel release. You'll feel truth. You'll begin to feel the weight lifting, and if you let it — you'll feel yourself becoming whole again.

Between the chapters, you'll find more than journal prompts. You'll find mirror talk, breathwork, meditations, coloring pages, emotional release exercises, and sacred space to cry, scream, write, reflect — and rise. This is more than a story. It's a soul work session in written form.

So, for the woman who lost her voice trying to keep the peace. For the woman who was strong until she snapped. For the woman who keeps getting up every single day in spite of — even when no one notices. For the woman who is ready to stop surviving and start becoming. This book is for you.

Take your time. Take deep breaths. Be honest, and when the healing starts to hurt just a little too much — come back to yourself, not your past. We're not chasing who we used to be here. We're becoming the woman we were always meant to be.

Let's begin.

Disclaimer: *This book is a tool for emotional reflection, self-discovery, and healing. It is not a substitute for professional therapy, mental health treatment, or advice from a licensed medical provider. If you are experiencing severe emotional distress, trauma, or mental health concerns, please seek support from a licensed therapist or counselor.*

TABLE OF CONTENTS

The Day I Buried HER

The version of me that kept surviving had to die so I could start living.

"She wasn't weak—she was just tired of surviving in a world that kept asking her to shrink. So she buried the version of herself who kept saying 'yes' when her spirit was screaming 'no'."

I remember the day I buried her like it just happened yesterday. Not with flowers. Not with tears. But with silence and truth, and honesty.

She was the version of me that said "I'm fine" while falling completely apart on the inside. The one who took the blame just to keep the peace. The one who made herself small in rooms where she deserved to shine. She lived in survival mode for so long, she forgot what peace even felt like. She forgot what being her truly meant.

I buried her when I finally admitted... That being the "strong one" was killing me. That constantly proving my worth was draining my soul. That loving people who didn't love me back was not noble – it was self-betrayal.

She served her purpose. She held me down through storms I thought would break me. She was the version of me who carried pain so I could smile through it, and I honor her for that. But I couldn't take her with me into this next chapter.

Because healing required something she didn't know how to give: Boundaries. Wholeness. Power. Peace.

The woman I am now – she don't beg. She don't chase. She don't explain. She knows her worth and walks in it. Daily. Loudly. Bold and in Truth. She knows that letting go isn't weakness, It's wisdom. If you're reading this and feeling like you've lost yourself, I want you to know that it's okay to grieve the version of you that kept it all together. It's okay to miss her, but it's time to let her go. Because the woman you're becoming needs more space to breathe. She needs space to flourish mentally, physically, spiritually, and emotionally. She doesn't belong in survival mode anymore. She's not coming back – and that's your super power.

Affirmation

I buried her with love. I rose with power.

Sis,

Don't rush through this. This is only the beginning as you have just begun digging up those roots. A lot of emotions will be evoked as you go through this process of self-love, and healing. It's going to get messy. It will definitely bring up bad memories. It' going to revive old wound. Insert old grievances. In those moments you will cry, you will feel indifferent, you will have so many questions. You'll even ask yourself why? You might cry so much it becomes hard to breathe. You might scream so loud your head hurts. But this will be your breakthrough moment. It's your time.

This book will help you get it all out. The parts you hated about her. The parts you loved about her. The things you never got to say. The things you wish someone else had said. I want you to sit in it, own it, and when you are done grieving— release it. The pain will only be temporary but the results will be amazing. As you go through this, my thoughts and prayers are with you. I'll be right here cheering you on every step of the way. Just know that I too had to do the work. It wasn't easy, and oh my-how I have grown throughout this process. This book is a testament to my healing. My wish is that it to will it be yours.

You have to make sure going through this process that you are always honest with your feelings and with yourself no matter how hard it gets. Let it all fall onto these pages. Grieve her. Honor her. Release her. When you're ready... bury her.

WELCOME

A Gentle Introduction to Your Healing Journey.

Sometimes before we can dig deep, we need to come up for air. This is a soft icebreaker to round up this chapter. Let this be the moment you greet yourself honestly — with no pressure, no pretending.

Who Are You Today?

- If I had to describe how I feel in one word, it would be: ________________
- Today, I'm showing up as someone who: ________________________
- One thing I'm proud of myself for surviving is: ____________________
- Something I wish someone would say to me right now is: ______________

What I'm Ready to Let Go Of?

- A version of me I've outgrown: _________________________
- A belief I'm ready to bury: ___________________________
- A role I no longer want to play: ________________________
- A fear that doesn't belong to me anymore: __________________

What I'm Giving Myself Permission For

- I give myself permission to feel: ________________________
- I give myself permission to stop: ________________________
- I give myself permission to grow into: _____________________
- I give myself permission to grieve and still be: _________________

This is your warm-up. This is your mirror. This is your safe return to yourself.

YOUR JOURNEY
SHAPES YOUR STORY.

Sis.... Check In!

What parts of yourself have you outgrown but are still holding on to?

When did you first realize you were just pretending to be ok?

What did the old you need that she never received?

Who will she become now - and what does she no longer tolerate?

CHAPTER REFLECTION - HOW ARE YOU FEELING?

CONTINUE

I Loved Him More Than He Ever Planned To Love Me

You can't teach someone to love you while they're actively unlearning your worth.

I called it love. He called it convenient. I stayed. He drifted. I broke. He barely noticed.

There's a specific kind of heartbreak that comes from loving a man who was never emotionally available, but you kept showing up anyway. I've been there, and I hated it.

I've cried in bathrooms while pretending everything was okay in front of friends. I've written texts I never sent, poured my soul into messages just to get one-word replies. I've convinced myself that he just needed time, that he was broken, that maybe if I just loved him harder, he'd see me.

But here's what I learned – and it nearly broke me before it healed me: You cannot force someone to love you properly. You can't earn a love that was never offered in the first place. You can't fill a man's empty cup if he keeps pouring yours out with his silence, his absence, his emotional unavailability, his non-communication, his distance.

Sis, read that again.

I used to think that if I became the perfect woman – the one who ran when he called, listened, supported, showed up, forgave too fast – he'd finally wake up and say, "You're the one." But all I did was lose myself trying to become worthy in someone else's eyes. He saw my softness, but he didn't respect it. He felt my love, but he didn't honor it. He took what I gave while never intending to give me anything in return.

It took me years to realize that I was always enough – he just wasn't capable. Or willing. Here's the part that changed me: His inability to love me was never my failure. It wasn't that I wasn't good enough – it's that he was never meant to be the one. So to the woman who's still waiting for a "What are we?" text... or a "Where Do We Go From Here?" reply. To the woman making excuses for why he doesn't call back, why he won't commit, why he keeps coming and going. Why are my feelings being made to feel invalid? The gas-lighting, narcissistic behavior. Constantly questioning yourself of what you can do better, how you can show up more, how can you make him love you. Stop. Stop it right now. You deserve better. You are worth so much more, and you know it.

The moment I stopped chasing love and started choosing myself, everything shifted. Because now – I don't compete for anyone's attention. I realized I am the prize. I am the peace. I am the love. Hey, if he couldn't see that, he was never my match.

Affirmation

“I don’t chase love. I choose myself — and that’s enough.”

Hey Sis

I bet this chapter felt like you got run over by an 18 wheeler. It definitely cost me a few tears letting these sack of bones resurface. Some things I thought I buried, I only suppressed. Things I thought I let go, until I had to bring them to the surface. It hurts like hell. Some of that pain dwelled in some pretty dark spaces. But I had to break all over again, just to piece myself back together. I needed to come up for air. Most importantly, I needed you to know my truth. I knew I had to keep going no matter how hard it got. I know some of these things will stir up emotions. Those many nights you stayed up waiting for them call, or come home. The questions left unanswered. The pieces of yourself you gave without question. Only to leave you brokenhearted, hurt and confused. But this is your release.

Write the letter you never sent. Say what you needed to say. Mourn the love you thought would last. Cry if needed. We have all had that love that just made us feel like the world disappeared when they were around. Only to have it come crashing back down on you when they no longer were. I can’t begin to tell you about the many nights I cried. Time for you to let it all out. Feel every single emotion in this moment. This is the time for you to finally say I’m over it. I’m done and I release it. This was never mine to carry in the first place. Then breathe.

Now begin writing the love story you’re finally giving yourself - the one where you are the center, the peace, the priority. You never needed him to complete you. You, just needed the strength to remember who you are. Now it’s time for you to add tax plus interest to your worth. You deserve it, and you are damn sure worth it.

GUIDED MEDITATION

"Releasing What I Was Never Meant To Carry"

- Find a quiet space. Sit upright or lie down comfortably. Let your hands rest softly on your belly or heart.

- Close your eyes and take a deep breath. Inhale through your nose... Hold...Exhale slowly through your mouth.

- Now, in your mind's eye, picture yourself standing at the edge of a calm river. You're holding a small satchel — heavy with stones. Each stone carries a name, a memory, a moment that hurt: the love that never loved you back... the words they never said...the effort they never returned... the questions you never got answered.

- One by one, take a stone and toss it into the water.

- As it disappears beneath the surface, say: "This was never mine to carry. I release it now. I release them now. I return to me."

- Keep breathing.

- Stay here for as long as you need. Let the water hold what your heart no longer can.

- When you're ready, slowly open your eyes.

- Place your hand back over your heart and whisper, "I am still here. I am whole. I am free."

Sis.... Check In!

When was the moment you realized he didn't love you like you deserved?

____

____

____

____

In what ways did you betray yourself to keep the relationship alive?

Yyhytÿ

____

____

____

____

What did you think love was supposed to feel like - and where did that belief come from?

____

____

____

____

How will you show up for yourself differently moving forward?

____

____

____

____

CHAPTER REFLECTION - HOW ARE YOU FEELING?

CONTINUE

Even Blood Can Be Toxic

Peace over people.
Even the ones you share DNA with.

"Just because we share blood doesn't mean I owe you access to my peace."

Let's me talk about being the "go-to" person in a family who doesn't respect your boundaries. They love you when you're saying yes. They celebrate you when you're useful. They expect you to show up, to give, to help, to drop everything for them – even if they haven't done a single thing for you in return. I used to carry that role like it was my birthright. I never said "NO." Not because I didn't want to – but because I knew the moment I did, the chaos would start. The side-eyes. The backhanded comments. The same old, "Hmm, she act like I owe her something," or "She always got an attitude."

But here's the truth they'll never say out loud: It's not my attitude that changed. It's my boundaries. It's not that I don't love them – I just stopped letting them use that love as a weapon. It's exhausting to keep showing up for people who only show up when it benefits them. To go to every party, every event, every baby shower – knowing full well they won't come to yours. To give, support, and uplift people who turn around and speak sideways about your name, your kids, your mother... behind your back.

And for what? Because we share blood?

No. Because they thought I was weak. Because I didn't speak up. Because I kept coming back. Because I forgave too easily. They mistook my love for foolishness. They thought kindness meant access. But now they're learning – the hard way – that I don't owe anyone access to my energy, my time, or my space, or my peace. I love hard. That's never changed. But now, I love me hard too. That means I don't go where I'm tolerated – I go where I'm cherished. Remember everyone has a story, you just have a lot of people who live in glass houses forgetting the stones they throw can be tossed back.

My little family and I... we stick together. We mind our business. We take care of our own. We don't talk about people just to feel better about ourselves. We sure as hell don't need anyone's validation of who they think we should be.

So if that makes us the black sheep – then baby, baaaa. I'd rather be the black sheep in peace than the favorite in fake spaces.

Affirmation

I don't owe anyone access to me just because we share the same last name and blood.

Sis,

I know this one hit different. The guilt of stepping back from family is heavy. We are raised to believe that blood means everything. But here's the truth: love without respect is just manipulation. Am I right?

This is your permission to stop pretending. To stop showing up in rooms where your name is used as a punchline. To protect your peace even if they call you selfish. You are not here to be the emotional mule for people who never pour back into you. I could give you some stories about some of the things that I have heard family say about me. They always bare their souls to the ones they think will never run back to say anything to you. But then for the ones who come back to tell you everything that was said, you have to question their intentions as well. What did you do in those moments when my name was being dragged? Did you stick up for me? Did you defend me in my absence. Or, did you willingly participate in the gossip, but decided to beat someone else to the punch to tell me what they said, so the finger wouldn't be pointed back at you? Even family has motives.

Remind yourself - your peace is sacred. If you are not for or of me, I know how to exit stage left. DEUCES! Hey, guess what? It doesn't require an apology either. Looking around my space as I casually sip my tea. Hello somebody!

BREATHWORK EXERCISE

"I Am Safe, I Am Grounded, I Am Enough"

Sometimes the people who share your blood are the ones who bleed you the most. When you've spent years being the "strong one," the "reliable one," the "never-says-no one"... your nervous system forgets what safety feels like. Let's come home to your body.

The 4–4–6 Grounding Breath

- Sit or lie down. Close your eyes.
- Place one hand on your belly, the other on your chest.
- Take a slow, deep breath inhaling through your nose for 4 counts.
- Hold your breath for 4 counts.
- Exhale gently through your mouth for 6 counts.

Repeat this for 3 to 5 rounds.

As you breathe, say quietly in your mind: "I am safe." "I am grounded." "I am enough."

Let every breath remind your body: You do not owe access to anyone who drains you. You are allowed to protect your peace — even from people who raised you. You are allowed to choose you.

Sis.... Check In!

In what ways have you felt unseen or taken advantage of by family?

What does loyalty look like to you, and have you been given it to people who don't reciprocate?

Where in your life do you need to protect your peace more fiercely?

How does it feel to walk away from spaces that only want your presence, not your well-being?

CHAPTER REFLECTION - HOW ARE YOU FEELING?

CONTINUE

She Was The Strong Friend Until She Wasn't

Being everything for everyone left nothing for me.

Everyone checked on me... once I stopped answering calls.

I've always been "the strong one." The one who listens. The one who shows up. The one people call at 2 a.m. when they're falling apart – because they know I'll answer. I always answer.

But here's the part they don't talk about... Who checks on the strong friend? Who notices when her silence is louder than her laughter? Who reaches out when her energy feels off? Who sees her when she's hiding in plain sight?

The truth is, I got so used to being needed that I forgot what it felt like to be nurtured. I'd be drowning – and still stretching my arms out to lift someone else up. I would smile through breakdowns, host ladies events, show up for everyone else, and give advice while silently praying someone would just ask me, "How are you really doing?" But noone ever did. Because strong friends don't break... right? Wrong. I broke quietly, and nobody noticed. Not because they didn't care – but because I had trained them not to. I had taught the world to expect my strength and hide my softness. To take, and never ask if I had anything left. But the worst part? I did it to myself. I stayed silent. I pushed my pain down.

I kept saying "I'm good" when I was anything but. Then one day... I just stopped. Stopped answering calls. Stopped showing up. Stopped giving strength I no longer had. You know what happened? Some people disappeared. Some were offended. Some even got mad at me – for not being who I had always been for them. But the ones who stayed? The ones who saw me even when I was low, who didn't need my strength to feel connected? Those were the ones I kept. They are the ones who deserve the best version of me, because they saw me at my worse and lifted me up when I needed them most. I love my tribe, they know who they are. What's understood, needs no explanation

Being the strong friend shouldn't mean you suffer in silence. Now, I still love hard. I still show up. But not at the expense of myself. I've learned that I am allowed to fall apart. I am allowed to need help. I am allowed to not be okay. The people who really love me? They'll hold space for me even when I have nothing left to give. They will love me in spite of it all.

Affirmation

I no longer perform strength to be worthy of love.

Hey Sis,

You don't always have to be the one holding everyone together. You don't always have to be the shoulder, the support, or the solid one all the time.

You are allowed to rest. To cry. To say "I'm not okay."

Release that load immediately. That's a weight that can be extremely overwhelming. When you don't have energy to give, and everyone gives you their energy and emotions, what does that do to you? Light bulb moment....that load can become colossal, even catastrophic for you. I'm tired just thinking about it. Energy cannot be created, or destroyed. But it can be transferred from one place to another. That can do a lot to the body, mentally, physically, spiritually, and emotionally.

You are allowed 100% to need and require the same love you give. You can't pour from an empty cup. I send you love and light during these moments. Take all the time you need for yourself in order to re-center and calm your inner being.

STRENGTH REDEFINED

A Permission Slip to Be Human

You've been praised for how much you carry. But now? It's time to take inventory of what strength really means to you. "I used to think strength meant smiling through pain. Now I know strength also means asking for help, crying without shame, and knowing when to rest."

Reflect:

What have I been carrying that no one sees?

____

____

____

____

____

____

____

____

____

____

____

YOUR STRENGTH STATEMENT

Complete this sentence:

“I am strong because...”

____

____

____

____

____

____

Then say it out loud. Speak it until it feels real.

Being strong doesn’t mean being unbreakable. It means knowing you deserve to be held too it out loud.

Sis.... Check In!

Have you ever felt unseen while being there for everyone else?

What version of "strength" were you taught to become?

How do you show up for others - and how do you need others to show up for you?

What's one way you can release the "strong friend" mask and ask for support?

CHAPTER REFLECTION - HOW ARE YOU FEELING?

CONTINUE

The Friendships That Expired Because "I Grew"

You just stop holding onto what outgrew your soul.

"Some friendships aren't lost. They're released — because your soul got tired of being tolerated instead of treasured."

I used to think some friendships were forever. Especially the one I had since the 11th grade. Twenty years of memories, secrets, support, and struggle. I watched her go through everything – from heartbreak to motherhood, from the worst days of her life to the ones she swore she'd never survive, and I was always there.

But she wasn't always there for me. She always forgot my birthdays. She didn't support my milestones. She rarely showed up unless it benefited her. When I got married, she treated my joy like it was an inconvenience – like my happiness was a betrayal of her pain. But truth be told... the signs and inconsistencies were there long before. I just didn't want to see them. I chose to love her in spite of it all.

I was the one giving. Always watching her kids. Planning the trips. Making space. Being a sister. What did I get in return? Lies. disrespect, and silence dressed as distance. I'll never forget when I took her on a trip for her High School graduation. She left me in Atlantic City with no explanation – just a call saying she was headed back with a man she had been dating that came to get her. It was like I didn't even matter. Like our friendship was disposable. However, we mended the friendship a few months after. Things seemed to be going well. But when people constantly show you who they really are, believe them. Years later she didn't just disappear – she started being nasty, dragging my name through the dirt. Telling lies. Trying to turn people against me. What did I do? I healed in silence. I cried. I grieved the loss. I let it break me for a season. Then I got up and kept it moving.

Six years later on a Facebook post my mother dedicated to me for my 40th, I finally received a "Happy Birthday". I said thank you. That's it. No anger. No shade. Just closure. Because I'm not in the business of forcing people to love me right. I don't need friends who only show up when it serves them. I don't need to clap for people who never clapped for me. I don't need people around me who dim my light just because theirs is flickering.

That friendship taught me that love without reciprocity is emotional exhaustion. That showing up for people who wouldn't do the same is self-harm in disguise. That sometimes, your biggest heartbreaks won't come from lovers – but from the women you called your sister, and that's okay. I send her love, light, and peace whenever I think of her. I made peace with the ending, and I've grown too much to fit back into something so small.

Affirmation

I release friendships that feel like obligation instead of love.

Hey Sis,

Losing a friend can feel just like a breakup — sometimes even deeper. It's a special kind of ache when the bond you once believed was unbreakable starts to unravel. Especially when it's someone you thought would always be part of your life. I'm real emotional right now. This has been such a process to get out. Lord knows I cried just as hard for a year straight after our friendship ended. For a while I resented her. But I had to go through to get through.

Those tears carried the weight of all the unspoken words, the unanswered texts, the birthdays they forgot. I grieved the laughter that echoed in our favorite memories, the inside jokes no one else would understand but us, the "remember whens" that now feel hollow, and the secrets between us that I still keep close.

Mourn the version of you who once settled for being tolerated instead of celebrated. The version that dimmed her light just to keep someone else comfortable. She deserves a goodbye too.

Write it all out — the truth, the pain, the confusion, the release. Let your ink say the things your heart never got to. Let your pen be the closure they never had the courage to give you. Let your healing roar louder than the silence they left behind. You don't have to hold malice — that only weighs you down.

Just hold yourself. Hold your heart with tenderness. Wrap yourself in the same love you so freely gave to them. While you're doing all of this remember to smile, because even though you may not believe it, somewhere out there, their still watching.

GROWTH OVER APPROVAL

When Friendships Expire Because You Grew.

Part 1: What I'm No Longer Shrinking For

Some friendships end not because of betrayal — but because of elevation. Growth reveals who was with you for who you were, not who you're becoming. And sometimes? The most painful goodbye is the one you never expected to say to a friend.

Reflect on the ways you've held yourself back to keep old friendships alive:

- I ignored my needs so I could ________________.
- I stayed small in my healing because I didn't want to ________________.
- I kept showing up even when I felt ____________________.

Part 2: When Friendship No Longer Feels Like Home

Think of a friend who once felt like family. Maybe they pulled away as you grew. Maybe you realized you were the only one holding the thread.

What did you learn about yourself through that friendship?

____

____

____

What boundaries or truths did this friendship teach you to honor?

____

____

____

Part 3: Goodbye Without Bitterness

Friendship breakups can feel heavier than romantic ones — because we never saw the ending coming. We thought they'd be there forever. We shared our secrets, our tears, our dreams. But sometimes, goodbye is the only way back to yourself.

Take a moment to write a letter to that friend — not to send, but to release. Speak your truth. No anger. Just peace.

Dear ________________,

____

____

____

____

____

____

____

____

Complete the sentence below as a final declaration:

"I may miss who we were, but I will never again abandon ________________ to keep someone beside me."

Letting go doesn't mean you're cold. It means you're clearing space for friendships that can meet you in your growth — not guilt you for it.

CHAPTER REFLECTION - HOW ARE YOU FEELING?

CONTINUE

You Can't Heal What You Keep Hiding

Your Silence is not strength. It's suffering in disguise.

"The soul will whisper until it breaks the body just to be heard."

I had my first stroke at 30 years old in 2007. Not from unhealthy eating. Not from partying. Not from reckless living. It came from something we don't talk about enough: emotional exhaustion, and stress. The second stroke came in 2008. The third... right after the pandemic in 2021. Three strokes. Three warning signs. Three wake-up calls. All of them happened while I was sitting behind a desk at a job. Let that sink in.

I was a mother of four. I had gone through a divorce. I was already grieving that love even after getting involved with someone else. After my second stroke, the man I had been with for five years just walked away. No phone call. No goodbye. Just gone. Abandonment hit me like a tidal wave. I felt discarded. Forgotten. Empty. I wasn't just hurting – I was drowning. The people I had always shown up for didn't even realize I was slipping.

I was still doing everything I could for everyone, while quietly falling apart. Until one day, I cracked. During a stupid argument with my mother, I grabbed a knife. In front of my mom. In front of my children, I tried to take my own life. I had reached the bottom. I was triggered. I wanted the pain to end. I wanted everything to stop. But then I heard a voice that saved me. My oldest daughter, with tears in her eyes, said: "I need you." "Who's going to be there when I get married? Who's going to help me raise my babies when I start my own family?" She also said something that still echoes in my soul till this very day... "Please, Mom... don't ever do that again." In that moment, I realized something... I had never given myself permission to 'FEEL'. I realized I was not okay, and I hadn't been for a long time.

That was the beginning of my real healing. I got help. I went to therapy. I finally admitted that I had been holding in pain that had no name – and when I got diagnosed with Major Depressive Disorder with Generalized Anxiety Disorder, I felt...free. Because now I could finally fight what I couldn't understand. That's the thing about pain. It festers in silence. You can't heal what you keep hiding. You can't recover from a wound you won't even look at. Now? I 'm on a journey I never thought I'd take. I take solo self-care trips. I cry. I journal. I laugh. I rest. I feel. I take myself on dates. I walk into spaces I used to think I wasn't allowed to enjoy with a smile. I don't wait for someone to save me anymore – because, I have learned how to save myself, every damn day. I don't pretend anymore. I don't pour from empty, and when I feel the heaviness creeping back in, I listen – before my body forces me to do so.

Affirmation

I give myself permission to stop pretending.
My healing starts with my honesty.

Sis,

Are you ok? I see you. I see the way you've been holding it all together, silently, while your world feels like it's crumbling. I see the strength you wear like armor — but I also see the cracks underneath. I need you to hear this from someone who has been where you are… It is okay to not be okay.

You don't have to fake the smile today. You don't have to say "I'm fine" when your spirit is screaming for someone to just notice. You're allowed to cry. You're allowed to feel tired. You're allowed to feel broken — because those feelings don't make you weak… they make you human.

Asking for help doesn't make you less. It doesn't make you fragile. It makes you powerful. It means that despite all you've been through, you're still believing in your right to rise. That right there is strength. That's a testament to the fight in you. That's the phoenix in you — wings covered in ash, heart still beating, flames still flickering, choosing to rise and live again.

Don't let this world tell you that your softness is a liability. It's a gift. Your vulnerability is your power. Your story — yes, even the messy parts — is your testimony. The moment you give yourself permission to tell the truth about your pain, you give another woman permission to heal as well. So if no one has told you today — I'm proud of you. For surviving. For showing up. For choosing life when everything in you wanted to give up. I stand with you. I cry with you. I celebrate you, and I promise… you're not alone anymore.

DRAW OUT YOUR ARMOR THEN REMOVE IT

We all build armor. We wear it in our silence, our smiles, our perfectionism, our people-pleasing. It kept us safe. It got us here. But we don't need it anymore.

Part 1: Describe Your Armor

- For the body outline below write what your armor has looked like: Guilt, overgiving, pretending to be okay, hiding your truth, shrinking to make others comfortable.

"This armor once protected me... but now it keeps me from fully being me."

Part 2: Replace the Armor with Freedom

Now, in the grid below, draw, doodle, or describe what freedom looks like without your armor: Peace, Boundaries, Joy, Authentic expression, Rest, Love that doesn't hurt.

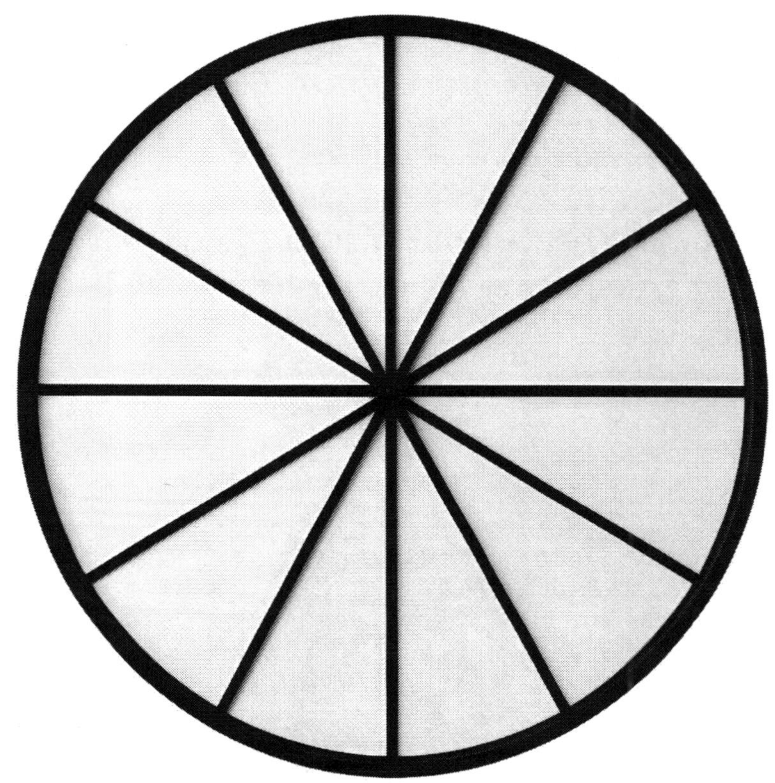

"This is who I am without the weight. This is what I wear now."

Reflect:

What has protecting yourself cost you?What has softening given you in return?
Write your truth here:

____

____

____

____

You are no longer at war with yourself. You don't have to earn safety. It lives in you now.

Sis.... Check In!

What pain have you been hiding from others - and from yourself?

What would it feel like to say, "I am not okay" and mean it?

What emotions have you buried to make others comfortable?

Who are you now that you've chosen to face your truth?

CHAPTER REFLECTION - HOW ARE YOU FEELING?

CONTINUE

Forgiving Myself For Not Knowing Better

Grace starts when guilt ends.

"I blamed myself for years for the things I didn't know… but how could I have done better, when I didn't know I deserved better?"

I used to beat myself up for the choices I made. For loving the wrong people. For staying too long. For ignoring red flags and painting them a prettier shade because I was so desperate for peace — I'd accept it, even if it came with pain. But the truth is, I was doing the best I could with the tools I had. I didn't have a blueprint. I didn't grow up watching women model soft, whole, self-loving boundaries. I watched women survive. I watched them endure. I watched them carry the world without ever being asked how they felt.

So that's what I became — a woman who thought endurance was love. A woman who thought her value came from how much she could take. A woman who didn't know that peace wasn't something you earned by breaking yourself down — it was something you were born worthy of, and when I finally hit that moment of awareness — when I saw how much I had allowed, how much I had accepted, how much I had given without receiving — I was angry. But not just at them. I was angry at me. Why didn't I walk away sooner? Why did I let them talk to me like that? Why did I give so much of myself and still end up feeling empty?

But that anger... it didn't heal me. It held me hostage. Because you cannot build a healed life on a foundation of self-blame. You can't shame yourself into becoming whole. You have to choose something softer. Something deeper. You have to choose forgiveness. Not for them — for you. Forgive the version of you who didn't know better. The version of you who thought love meant sacrificing your voice. The version of you who said "yes" out of fear and "I'm okay" out of survival. That version of you? She was doing everything she could with a heart that only ever wanted to be seen, heard, and loved. So I stopped punishing her. I stopped calling her foolish. I started telling her, "You did your best, baby girl. And now that we know better... we'll do better. Together."

Forgiveness is the doorway to freedom, and I walked through it — for me. You can, too.

Affirmation

"I forgive the woman I used to be — because she helped me become who I am now."

Sis,

You've carried enough guilt. Enough "I should've known," enough "why didn't I see it?" Enough shame dressed up as reflection. But today, I want you to lay it all down. It's not yours to carry anymore.

Talk to the woman you used to be. Hold her hand. Hug her. Speak to her with softness. Tell her: You didn't fail. You learned. You grew. You made it, and now… it's time to forgive her. Not because she was wrong — but because she was trying, and that matters more than anything. Remember you can't forgive anyone else, until you first forgive yourself. Besides, forgiveness isn't for them, it's for you.

TELL YOUR TRUTH

Finish this letter in your own words:

Dear Me,

I know it wasn't all them. I know I've made mistakes too...

____

____

____

____

____

____

____

____

____

But I'm ready to forgive the version of me who didn't know better. I'm ready to stop being the villain in my own life. Because healing starts with truth., and I'm telling mine now.

Reminder:

"The most powerful thing you can do is stop blaming the world and start rebuilding your soul. Not with shame. But with accountability, softness, and grace."

Sis.... Check In!

What decisions have you been silently blaming yourself for?

If you could speak to your past self without judgement, what would you say?

What beliefs were you taught about love, worth, or womanhood that no longer serve you?

How has self-forgiveness opened the door for you to grow?

CHAPTER REFLECTION - HOW ARE YOU FEELING?

CONTINUE

When You Realize You Are The Villain In Your Own Story

Healing starts the moment you stop pointing and start looking in the mirror.

"It's easier to say they hurt me. It's harder to admit I stayed. That I ignored the signs. That I kept choosing what was breaking me."

It's easy to tell the story in a way that makes you the victim, and maybe you were. Maybe they lied. Maybe they ghosted you. Maybe they cheated. Maybe they made you feel invisible in rooms you helped build. Maybe they took you for granted. Maybe they were incapable of love. Maybe they thought you were weak. But here's the part that not everyone's ready for: Sometimes the person you need to forgive... is you.

Because maybe you stayed too long. Maybe you knew deep down it wasn't love. Maybe you ignored your intuition over and over again just to say you had someone. Maybe you kept choosing people who were only ever there to teach you what you needed to heal – and then you turned around and blamed them for not staying.

I had to sit with that truth. I had to admit that I wasn't always the one who got hurt – sometimes, I was the one hurting myself. I was the one setting myself on fire just to keep someone else warm. The one over-explaining, over-loving, over-performing – hoping they'd finally see me. When they didn't... I told the world they did me wrong. But did I do me right? That's the question that rocked me to my core. I had to admit that some of the pain I carried didn't come from what they did – it came from what I allowed.

From the expectations I placed on people who never signed up to be what I needed. From the fact that I kept giving second, third, and tenth chances to people who showed me exactly who they were. I was mad at them... but deep down, I was disappointed in myself. That was a hard pill to swallow – but it was also the beginning of my liberation. Because the moment I owned my part, I got my power back. I stopped waiting for closure. I stopped needing apologies. I stopped replaying every wrong done to me and started asking, "Why did I make myself so small just to be chosen?" Let me tell you something... Once I held myself accountable with love – not shame – everything shifted. Because this isn't about beating yourself up. It's about freeing yourself.

You can't rewrite your story if you keep pretending you were only ever the hero. Sometimes you were the villain. Sometimes you were the lesson, and that's okay. You're not that version of you anymore. You've grown. You're healing, and now you're choosing better – because you know better.

Affirmation

"I forgive myself for the ways I let myself down — and I choose better from here."

Sis,

I know. It's hard to face the truth — especially when you've spent years telling yourself it was always someone else's fault. But here's the grace in it: you were learning. You weren't weak. You weren't dumb. You weren't broken. You were growing. You were surviving. You were showing up the only way you knew how.

Take this moment and be real with yourself. Sit in your the truth. The regrets. The lessons. The guilt. Then… forgive her. You can't change what happened — but you can change what you accept from this day forward, and that's power, sis. That's peace.

GRACE AND RELEASE

When Friendships Expire Because You Grew.

Part 1: I Didn't Know... But Now I Do

Write down a few truths about who you were then — and who you are becoming now.

- I didn't know that ______________________ was not love.
- I didn't know I was allowed to ________________________.
- I didn't know that healing would mean __________________________.
- I didn't know how to say no to _________________________.

"But now I know... and that's enough to begin again."

Part 2: Dear Me, I'm Sorry

Take a moment to write a short apology letter to the version of yourself who did the best she could with what she had.

Dear Me,

I'm sorry for...

____

____

____

I forgive you because...

____

____

Part 3: Grace Statements

Choose (or create) a few gentle reminders to carry with you:

- I give myself grace for not knowing then what I know now.
- I do not have to punish myself to prove I've grown.
- I am allowed to learn, evolve, and change.
- Forgiveness does not erase the past — it frees my future.
- I am worthy of softness, even from myself.

Write a few of your own here:

- ____
- ____
- ____
- ____
- ____

Forgiveness is how we return to ourselves. You are not behind. You are right on time.

Sis.... Check In!

What patterns have you repeated in your relationships that you now recognize as self-sabotaging?

____

____

____

____

When have you stayed in situations you knew wer hurting you - and why?

____

____

____

____

What truths about your role in your own pain are you ready to face, without judgement?

____

____

____

____

Who are you becoming now that you're choosing honesty over ego?

____

____

____

____

CHAPTER REFLECTION - HOW ARE YOU FEELING?

CONTINUE

Healing While Mothering

Raising babies while raising yourself is a silent kind of war.

"I didn't just carry my children. I carried my pain, my regrets, my exhaustion… and still made room to love them through it all."

I've been a mother since I was 15. Picture that! While other girls were being cheerleaders, playing sports, planning for college, living out their dreams, I was warming bottles and praying I didn't mess up the little life that depended on me. I wasn't ready — but I wanted to be loved. I thought having someone of my own would fill the emptiness. It was never easy.

I came home from school, fed and bathed my baby, tried to finish homework, and squeezed in small phone calls with my friends just to still feel like a teenager. Then baby number two came at 19. Then 21. Then 23. At the age of 23 I had four children and a ring on my finger — had to move halfway across the country to Colorado Springs, CO as a military wife, barely recognizing myself. I've experienced pain in every form: mental, emotional, physical. Through it all, I mothered. I'm not saying I was perfect, but I did the very best I could to give my kids a decent life.

Even when I smoked cigarettes to escape. Even when I wanted to disappear. Even when no one checked on me, because I was always the one who "had it together." But the truth? I wasn't healing — I was surviving.

As mothers, especially single mothers, we tuck our pain between lunchboxes and late-night laundry loads. We bleed silently. I'm 48 now and my kids are all fully grown living their best lives. I am a grandmother to a beautiful little girl who gives me just as much purpose as they did. But with her, she gets the healed, fulfilled person that my kids didn't get. She will have a healthy and loving relationship with me that is full of nothing but joy and laughter. It feels good to be able to spend time with her, giving her the life I so richly wanted to give them, while still trying to grow up myself. They all deserve the healed version of me more than the broken one I was trying to hide.

Now, when I laugh, when I take solo trips, when I cry freely without shame — my children and grandchild get to witness a woman returning home to herself. That's the legacy I want to leave. That's the healing they deserve to see.

Affirmation

I can love my children, and still choose to heal myself.

Sis,

You've done what most would've crumbled under. You've raised babies while carrying wounds. You've smiled when your heart was breaking. You've cooked dinner, wiped tears, paid bills, showed up at school events… all while silently screaming for someone to save you.

Cheers to the woman who mothered, weathered so many storms, broke and pieced herself back together. A hearty salute to the woman who is still taking it day by day to ensure she keeps it all together and not fall between the cracks. To the wounded woman behind the caregiver mask, if no one else tells you, I Love You. It's okay to be tired. It's okay to not have all the answers. It's okay to still be healing. You're not failing. You're just finally choosing yourself, too. That's the most powerful thing a mother can ever do.

MAMA MANTRAS

A Light and Loving Exercise for Mamas Healing in Real Time

These are affirmations to say when you're tired, overwhelmed, or feeling like you're falling short. Choose your favorites or write your own!

- I am a good mom — even on my hard days.
- My love is enough.
- I don't need to be perfect. I just need to be present.
- I am healing — and my children are watching me rise.
- Joy is allowed in my motherhood journey.

Write five of your own mantras below:

- ____
- ____
- ____
- ____
- ____

MAMAS HAPPY LIST

Healing doesn't always have to be heavy. Sometimes it's in the little moments that remind you who you are.

Fill this in with things that make you feel alive, relaxed, or simply YOU:

- A song that lifts my spirit: ______________________________
- A meal or treat that comforts me: ______________________
- A solo activity that recharges me: ______________________
- A scent that instantly soothes me: _______________________
- A time of day I feel most like myself: ______________________
- Something I love I want to return to: _____________________
- A movie that cheers me up: _____________________________
- A place where I feel completely at peace: ___________________
- A color that instantly lifts my mood: _______________________
- A place in nature I want to visit more often: _____________________
- A book or podcast that inspires me: ___________________________
- A quote that I love: ____
- A word or phrase I want to hear more often: _____________________

"I get to be both — healing and mothering. And I'm doing beautifully."

Sis.... Check In!

In what ways have you put your healing on hold to show up for others?

____

____

____

____

What do you wish someone had done for you while you were mothering through pain.

____

____

____

____

What version of motherhood were you taught - and how are you redefining it?

____

____

____

____

How would it feel to mother yourself with the same grace you give your children?

____

____

____

____

CHAPTER REFLECTION - HOW ARE YOU FEELING?

CONTINUE

Chapter 10 Relearning How To Love My Body

Self-love begins when you stop asking your body for permission to feel beautiful.

"I spent years shrinking, hiding, and apologizing for my body… until I remembered it was the only place I'd ever truly lived."

Motherhood is beautiful – but let's be honest... It will stretch you. Literally and figuratively. After carrying six babies and giving birth to four, my body had changed in ways I never expected. With every stretch mark, every pound gained, every "why can't I lose this weight?" moment – I lost a little more of myself. There were years I wouldn't even look in the mirror. I'd change with the lights off. Hell I even began hiding from my current husband. I'd throw on jeans, hoodies, sneakers – not because it was my style, but because I was hiding. I didn't feel sexy. I didn't feel seen. I'll be honest... there were times I was secretly envious of my friends – how they looked, how confident they seemed in their skin. It hurt. But I carried it like a silent sentence. I told myself, "This is just what happens when you're a mom. When you're depressed. When life just be lifing."

But this year... something shifted. My oldest daughter said something to me that stopped me in my tracks. She said, "You know what I started doing, Mommy? I force myself to look at myself naked in the mirror every day, and I tell myself, 'I look TF good.'" I said, "Girl, I know that's right." Crazy part is that girl isn't as big as a minute. Super gorgeous, tall and model-like. Just goes to show you that even people with little to no weight are just as judgmental and self-conscious about their bodies as us BBW's.

It was more than a moment. It was a mirror. A reminder that I can't love myself if I keep avoiding my reflection. That healing my relationship with my body means stripping down – not just physically, but emotionally. This body? It carried LIFE. It birthed four humans. It has survived trauma, sickness, stress, heartbreak, and still gets up every day and fights for me. These stretchmarks? They are art. They are proof. They are access to a sacred experience that some women only dream of. I'm not broken. I'm blessed. The best part is... if I don't like something, I can change it. I'm not stuck. I'm not hopeless. I just needed to remember I had options.

Now, I'm stepping into my soft girl era. I wear dresses. I wear color. I wear joy. I'm learning to feel myself, not just dress myself. What Remy Ma say? "I'm conceited – I got a reason." Period. But I'm super humble. I know I'm the full package – beauty, brains, brilliance, motherhood, entrepreneurship, and wisdom all wrapped up in one. Nobody can take that away from me. I am thankful. I am grateful. I am blessed, and baby, I look TF good doing it.

Affirmation

"My body is not broken — it's beautiful, it's blessed, and it's mine."

Sis,

I know you've struggled with your reflection. I know you've looked at your body and felt unworthy, unloved, or unseen. But you are absolutely gorgeous. You don't need validation. God made you in his perfect image. That's such a beautiful thing to know and witness.

But I want you to do something brave right now. Take this time to thank your body for all that it has done for you. Apologize to it. Celebrate it. It's been your home since birth. It's carried your children. Your pain. Your joy. It deserves to be loved — not after the weight is gone, not after the glow-up… but right now. In all its softness, stretchmarks and curves. All its strength. All its sacred power. You deserve to feel like the best version of yourself at all times. It doesn't matter what the world may see, or perceive you to be. How you feel and show up for yourself is what matters more than anything. Don't give that power away.

In every inch of your gorgeous existence, there is a story of a woman who has survived everything. This is your sacred skin. Treat it like holy ground.

BODY LOVE EXERCISE

Relearning How To Love The Skin You're In

Part 1: Body Brag Sheet

Let's flip the script. Forget shame. Forget comparison. Let's CELEBRATE this body. She's done a lot for you. Now you get to hype her up.

Fill in the blanks below with pride:

- My favorite body feature is: ______________________________
- The sexiest thing about me is: ______________________________
- I feel most powerful when I wear: ______________________________
- The part of my body that tells my story is: ______________________
- My body once did THIS amazing thing: _______________________
- My body feels most alive when: ______________________________
- When I look in the mirror I see: ______________________________
- This color compliments my skin: ______________________________
- When I walk into a room my energy says: ______________________________
- My favorite fragrance for my body is: ______________________________
- My skin feels like: ______________________________
- My stretch marks remind me: ______________________________
- I am most grateful that my body: ______________________________
- My smile says to the world: ______________________________
- I carry power in my: ______________________________
- My beauty is undeniable when: ______________________________
- My hips/thighs/curves/edges tell the story of: ______________________________

Bonus: Give your body a nickname! (Queen? Warrior? The Vessel?)
I call her: ____

Sis.... Check In!

What have you believed about your body that you now realize came from shame, not truth?

____

When was the last time you looked at yourself with love instead of critique?

What parts of your body have you been hiding, and what would it look like to embrace them?

How has motherhood, trauma, or life changed your relationship with your body?

CHAPTER REFLECTION - HOW ARE YOU FEELING?

CONTINUE

God, Are You Still With Me?

When you're silent, I wonder if You've left me—or if You're letting me find myself.

"I didn't stop believing in God. I just didn't know if He still believed in me."

I've had moments where I've sat in a dark room, eyes swollen from crying, fists clenched around prayers that felt like they went nowhere, and I'd whisper into the silence, "God... are You still with me?"

I didn't stop believing. I couldn't. But it got hard to feel Him when everything around me was breaking. Three strokes. A failed marriage. Abandonment. Financial pressure. Depression so thick it wrapped around me like fog. I was doing everything "right." Praying. Surviving. Loving. Giving. Yet it still felt like God had gone quiet. That silence hurt more than the pain sometimes. Because silence made me wonder: Did I do something wrong? Have I failed you? Am I no longer worthy of your presence, favor, and voice? I wanted signs. I wanted answers. I wanted to scream, "If you're here, say SOMETHING!"

But the truth is... It was in the silence that I began to hear "me". In the stillness, in the dark moments when I had no choice but to sit with my wounds, I found something deeper than shouting faith — I found surrendered faith. Faith didn't need everything to make sense. Faith that said, "Even if I don't hear You, I will still trust You." Faith that rose up from the ashes of my breakdowns and said, "I'm still here, and if I'm still here... You must be too."

God never left me. He was there in the arms of my daughter when she said, "I need you." He was there when my lungs filled up again after another panic attack. He was there when I woke up and decided to try one more time. Sometimes, God doesn't show up the way we expect — with lightning bolts and loud deliverance. Sometimes, He shows up in our resilience. In the fact that we're still standing. And now? I don't ask, "God, are You still with me?" I say, "Thank You for holding me when I forgot how to pray." Because I know... He never left. Not once.

Affirmation

"Even in silence, I am held. God never left me — not even for a second."

Sis,

I know what it feels like to wonder if God is still listening… if he still sees you… If he's forgotten your name in a world that feels like it keeps forgetting your worth. I've been there — face down, crying into my pillow, silently begging for a sign. A whisper. Anything to let me know I wasn't alone.

Sometimes the silence makes you question everything. But I need you to know this truth — not just in your head, but in your heart: He never left. Not when the marriage failed. Not when your health declined. Not when you lost yourself trying to be everything for everyone. Not when you whispered prayers with no words left. God wasn't punishing you. He was preserving you. You didn't go through the fire to be forgotten. You went through it so the ashes could reveal the woman you're becoming — bold, wise, soft, and strong. You're not too far gone. You're not too broken. You're not too late.

So talk to Him. Not with perfect words. Just real ones. Tell Him the truth about your fears, your doubts, your anger — He can handle all of it. And when you're done… be still. Because even in the quiet, you are held.
He hasn't left. Not once. He's been waiting for you to come home to him… and to yourself.

A WOMAN'S PRAYER

For the woman who's faith is flickering but not gone.

Heavenly Father,

Sometimes I whisper this question into the dark: "God, are You still with me?" Because there are days I feel so distant, so discouraged, so done.
But today, I come back to You. Not perfect. Not polished. Just honest.
Your Word says, ***"The Lord is close to the brokenhearted and saves those who are crushed in spirit." (Psalm 34:18)*** — so here I am, crushed but calling.

When my faith feels like it's slipping through my fingers, remind me that ***"Faith is the substance of things hoped for, the evidence of things not seen". (Hebrews 11:1)*** When I feel indifferent, wrap me in ***"Your peace that surpasses all understanding". (Philippians 4:7)*** When I feel empty, ***"Restore to me the joy of Your salvation". (Psalm 51:12)*** When I feel weak, let me remember: "But those who hope in the Lord will renew their strength. ***"They will soar on wings like eagles." (Isaiah 40:31)"***

God, teach me how to walk again — even when I can't see the path. Let me rise with confidence each morning, knowing I do not walk alone. Give me wisdom to say "no" to anything that threatens my peace. Give me discernment to walk away from what isn't sent by You. Give me strength to forgive those who've wished harm upon me — and courage to release them completely. Protect my heart from bitterness. Protect my mind from confusion. Protect my soul from settling. Replace my doubt with destiny. Replace my fear with fire. Replace my silence with prayer.

God, remind me that even in the silence, You are still working. Even in the wilderness, You are still leading. Even in my weariness, you are still my strength.
I may bend. I may break. But I will not be buried here. Because you, Lord, are still with me, and because of you, so am I.

In Jesus' name, Amen.

Sis.... Check In!

Have you ever felt abandoned by God? What was happening in your life at the time?

____

____

____

____

What prayers have you stopped praying because you lost hope in the answer?

____

____

____

____

In what ways has God show up silently - through people, moments, or unexpected strength?

____

____

____

____

What does faith look like for you now in your healing session?

____

____

____

____

CHAPTER REFLECTION - HOW ARE YOU FEELING?

CONTINUE

I’m Not Angry, I’m Just Done

Closure isn’t a conversation — it’s a decision.

"I didn’t stop loving you. I just stopped breaking myself to be understood by someone who never planned to see me."

There’s a difference between being angry… and being done. Anger is loud. It fights. It tries to fix. It still wants something back. But being done… Done is quiet. Done doesn’t beg. Done doesn’t explain. Done doesn’t send one more paragraph just to be heard.

I’ve had to learn the art of release without bitterness. Because some people will never say sorry. Some people will never tell the truth. Some people will never see the pain they caused — because that would require them to admit they were wrong. Accountability isn’t something everyone is ready for. I used to try to “fix” things with people who were perfectly fine, leaving me confused, drained, and in the dark. I’d send the long text. Try to “talk it out.” Give chance after chance. But what I didn’t realize then is that closure doesn’t come from them — it comes from me.

You don’t need one more apology. You don’t need them to “get it.” You just need to permit yourself to walk away from what’s no longer aligned with your peace.

Now!! I don't argue. I don’t chase conversations that don’t pour into me. I don’t throw pearls where they’ll be stepped on. I release with love. With quiet. With clarity. I’m not angry. I’m not bitter. I’m not pressed. I’m just done. Because peace feels better than being “right.” Because protecting my energy is more important than proving my point. Because healing has taught me that not every door needs to be slammed — some just need to stay closed.

If they ever wonder why you don’t reach out anymore? Why your energy shifted? Why you stopped explaining yourself or making space at tables where you were only ever tolerated — let them wonder. Because this version of you doesn’t owe them anything. Not a warning. Not a breakdown. Not a return. Walking away is the closure. Choosing yourself is peace. And sometimes the loudest healing you’ll ever do… is the silence after goodbye.

Affirmation

"I don't need closure. I need peace — and I choose it every time."

Sis,

You don't have to fight anymore. You don't have to keep rehearsing your pain to people who never really listened. You don't need to chase closure from those who were okay watching you break. You're allowed to be done.

Not angry. Not petty. Not bitter. Just… done.

Take the time to speak your goodbye letter you never sent. The conversation you've outgrown. The things you've screamed in silence but never released. Then take a breath. Not because it's over for them… But because it's finally over for you.

This is you reclaiming your time, and your peace. You don't lose love for people, you just lose the patience to tolerate what they were constantly giving you. People take advantage of those they never think will walk away until they finally do. Oh well, it's their loss. It's a miserable feeling for people when they realize just how bad they fumbled a good person. Sometimes you gotta throw them three fingers up and tell them to read between the lines. You feel me?

RELEASE WITHOUT APOLOGY

A Soulful Check-In to Help You Honor Your Quiet Exit

Part 1: My Peace Inventory

This is the season where you choose stillness over chaos. No more over-explaining. No more forcing conversations. Just peace — sacred, quiet, unwavering peace.

Fill in what you've quietly walked away from.

- A relationship that no longer honors me: ______________________________
- A space where I always felt drained: ________________________________
- A habit or mindset that robbed me of peace: ___________________________
- An expectation I've stopped trying to meet: ____________________________

Part 2: The Quiet Exit

Not every goodbye needs a grand finale. Sometimes the most powerful thing you can do is leave silently and let them wonder why.

Reflect on this prompt:

"I didn't announce my exit because..."

____

____

____

____

____

____

____

Now complete this release:

"I left not to hurt you, but to protect me. I'm no longer angry — I'm just unavailable.

PPart 3: Done Doesn't Mean Cold

Being done doesn't mean you don't care. It means you care too much about yourself to keep bleeding for people who won't even notice you're cut.

Complete these truths:

- Done feels like: ______________________________
- Done sounds like: ______________________________
- Done looks like: ______________________________
- Done allows me to finally: ______________________________
- Done gives me back my: ______________________________
- Done is not a weakness, it is: ______________________________
- Done is me choosing: ______________________________
- Done is what peace whispered when: ______________________________
- Done no longer seeks: ______________________________
- Done taught me that silence can be: ______________________________
- Done allowed me to see who really: ______________________________
- Done helped me stop performing for: ______________________________
- Done is walking away from what: ______________________________
- Done is walking toward what: ______________________________
- Done is no longer apologizing for: ______________________________
- Done reminds me that self-love looks like: ______________________________
- Done is not the end, it's the: ______________________________
- Done is me choosing myself over: ______________________________
- Done taught me I can love from: ______________________________

It means you care too much about yourself to keep bleeding for people who won't even notice you're cut.

"Being done isn't about bitterness. It's about boundaries. And baby, mine are blessed and guarded now."

Sis.... Check In!

What are you holding onto out of obligation or guilt that you're truly done with?

____

____

____

____

How has trying to be understood kept you stuck in cycles that drain you?

____

____

____

____

What would it feel like to release someone or something without anger - just peace?

____

____

____

____

What does being done look like in your life right now?

____

____

____

____

CHAPTER REFLECTION - HOW ARE YOU FEELING?

CONTINUE

The Burnout I Never Admitted

You don't have to collapse to deserve rest.

"I wasn't lazy. I wasn't unmotivated. I was burned out — emotionally, spiritually, and soul-deep."

There's a different kind of tired that sleep doesn't fix. It's the kind of tired you feel in your bones. In your spirit. In the space between your smiles. For the longest time... I ignored it. I kept going. Kept pushing. Kept performing strength like it was a requirement. I thought that slowing down meant I was weak. That asking for help made me look incapable. That rest was something you earned, not something you deserved by simply being human. But sis... I was exhausted, and I didn't even know it.

I had learned how to operate on empty. To show up for everyone but myself. To make things look good on the outside while falling apart internally. Smiling for my family. Showing up for work. Answering calls. Encouraging others. Meanwhile... nobody knew I was slipping. The hardest part was that I had no idea how to say I'm tired without feeling guilty for it.

I was taught to be strong, to push through, to wear resilience like a badge of honor — even when it was costing me everything. Burnout doesn't always look like falling apart. Sometimes it looks like you quietly disappearing from yourself. I wasn't lazy. I wasn't broken. I was burned out. Soul-deep.

When I finally admitted it — when I whispered, "I can't keep living like this" — I didn't crumble. I breathed. Because naming it gave me power. Acknowledging it gave me freedom. Now, I don't wait for breakdowns. I schedule rest. I prioritize silence. I pour back into me. Because I've learned that rest is not a luxury. It's a boundary. It's survival. It's sacred.

Affirmation

"My rest is not a reward — it's a requirement."

Sis,

If you've been tired… truly, deeply, soul-weary tired — I want you to know that you're not lazy. You're not failing. You're not weak. You're burned out.

You don't need anyone's permission to rest. This page is your time to tell the truth — about the weight you've been carrying, the expectations you've been trying to meet, the parts of you that are screaming for relief. Cry if you need to. Say the words you've been swallowing.

Then promise yourself this: I will never again apologize for resting. I will never again abandon myself for the sake of being "strong." I don't need to earn peace. I just need to protect it.

TALK TO HER –SHE DESERVES TO HEAR IT

Mirror Talk Prompt: "I Deserve Loyalty That Matches My Heart"

- Go stand in front of your mirror. No filter. No makeup. No pretending. Just you — and your reflection.

- Place your hands over your heart and breathe. Now say this out loud: "You are not to blame for their betrayal. You didn't lose a friend. You lost a one-sided story. You are not hard to be loyal to — they just didn't know how to love without conditions."

- Look into your own eyes. Even if it stings. Even if your voice shakes. Say: "I see you. I trust you. And I will never let anyone make you question your worth again."

Let it land. Let it echo. Let it heal.
You are not alone. You just got your space back.

Sis.... Check In!

In what areas of your life have you been running on empty?

What messages were you given about rest, strength, and self-sacrafice?

How has burnout shown up in your body, your energy, or your emotions?

How can you start building a life that includes rest as a part of your routine?

CHAPTER REFLECTION - HOW ARE YOU FEELING?

CONTINUE

My Boundaries Are Not Up For Debate

If it costs my peace, it's too damn expensive.

"I used to explain my boundaries. Now I enforce them. That's not rudeness — that's growth."

There was a time when I made excuses for my "no." When I over-explained why I couldn't show up, why I wasn't answering the phone, why I was unavailable to pour into someone else when I was running on fumes. Because deep down, I didn't want to seem mean. I didn't want to disappoint anybody. I didn't want people to think I'd changed.

But here's what I finally learned: You're allowed to change. You're allowed to grow out of people-pleasing. You're allowed to stop letting people have access to you just because they're used to it. That's the very reason why we set boundaries. Not walls. Not punishments. Not shade.

Boundaries are love for yourself. They are the bold, quiet way of saying, "I matter too." I used to let people walk all over me in the name of "being nice." Let them drain me, disrespect me, and still show up like I wasn't dying inside. I thought being selfless was love. But I've learned — if the only way to keep someone is to betray myself, that ain't love... that's manipulation.

Now, I don't explain my boundaries — I enforce them. I don't second-guess what makes me uncomfortable. I don't justify my need for space, silence, or separation. If they don't like it, that's okay. Because I'm not shrinking anymore just to be digestible. I'm not setting myself on fire just to keep everyone else warm. I'm not available for guilt trips, emotional manipulation, or entitled expectations. This version of me chooses peace — every single time. If that makes me "different," then baby... thank God I'm not who I used to be.

Affirmation

**My boundaries are non-negotiable.
Protecting my peace is my responsibility**

Sis,

You don't have to be everything to everyone. You don't have to overextend, overexplain, or overcompensate to be loved. You are not selfish for choosing rest. You are not rude for saying no. You are not cold for protecting your heart.

Take the time to figure out what boundaries you need to set — with friends, family, lovers, and even yourself.

Say the things you've been holding in. Reclaim your time, your space, your energy. Because when you set a boundary, you're not pushing people away. You're inviting peace in.

And sis — you deserve all the peace.

THE OPEN + CLOSED DOOR

Boundaries are not walls to keep everyone out — they're doors that remind you who and what gets access to the sacred space within you.

Let's decide what enters... and what stays outside.

Open Door (What I Now Welcome In)

Write what you are inviting into your life, space, and energy:

I now welcome relationships that feel: ______________________________
I now allow myself to say yes to: __________________________________
I give full permission to receive: _________________________________
I feel safe with people who: ____________________________________

Closed Door (What I Now Refuse to Entertain)

Write what you are no longer available for:

I close the door on people who: _____________________________________
I no longer tolerate energy that feels: ______________________________
I refuse to explain myself when: ___________________________________
I revoke access from anyone who: __________________________________

Boundary Reclaiming Script

Fill in the blanks to practice speaking your truth with love and firmness:

"This version of me doesn't do ___________________ anymore. If that doesn't work for you, I respect your path — but I'll be protecting mine."

"Every boundary I create is a declaration of my worth. And baby, it's not up for debate."

"Every time you choose your peace over pleasing, your truth over tolerance, and your healing over history — you build a boundary. And that boundary is sacred."

Sis.... Check In!

Where in your life have your boundaries been ignored - and how did that make you feel?

What's one of your boundaries you've been afraid to set out of fear of disappointing someone?

What beliefs were you taught to make you feel guilty for choosing yourself?

How does it feel to know you have the right to protect your energy without apology?

CHAPTER REFLECTION - HOW ARE YOU FEELING?

CONTINUE

Chapter 15

Peace Is My New Love Language

Peace is not the absence of chaos - it's the presence of self-love.

"I didn't know how much peace I needed until I finally started prioritizing it."

For a long time, I mistook chaos for love. If it didn't come with drama, intensity, or a little heartbreak, I thought it wasn't real. I craved passion — the kind that pulled me in, kept me guessing, made my heart race... and my soul ache. But baby, that wasn't love. That was emotional addiction. That was me being used to instability, so anything consistent felt boring. That was me calling anxiety "chemistry." That was me confusing a rollercoaster for a relationship.

But I've healed too much to go back to that. I don't want chaos anymore. I don't want the kind of love that makes me question myself, compete for attention, or pour into someone who can't hold space for my softness. Now? Peace is my new love language. I want presence. I want comfort. I want to be able to sit in silence and still feel seen. I want to be around people — friends, family, etc. — who feel like peace. The older I get, the more I realize... I don't need loud. I need safe. I don't need constant excitement. I need alignment. I don't need to be chased — I need to be respected.

Peace doesn't mean my life is perfect. It just means I'm no longer addicted to the pain that came with people who couldn't love me right. Now I guard my peace like a sacred ritual. Because the woman I am today knows that peace isn't boring — it's everything.

Affirmation

"I don't chase intensity anymore. I choose peace — in people, in places, in love, and in me."

Sis,

I know what it's like to mistake tension for passion. To believe that love should come with emotional highs and lows, like a storm you survive over and over again. I know what it's like to think the love that made you cry then they must have been the one worth fighting for, because at least it felt intense. At least it felt real. I also know what it's like to sit in stillness and feel uncomfortable — to confuse peace with boredom, because you were so used to chaos.

But let me tell you something with my whole heart: That wasn't love. That was survival speaking. That was trauma bonding. That was emotional exhaustion masquerading as connection. Real love? It doesn't make you second-guess your worth. It doesn't require you to earn rest, safety, or softness.

Peace is your inheritance. You deserve to be held in a way that doesn't hurt. You deserve to sit beside someone—even if that someone is you, and breathe without bracing for pain. Use this space to redefine love. To remember that peace isn't passive — it's powerful.

Stillness is power. Safety in secure. Know what real connection — rooted in calm and care — means to the woman you're becoming. Speak softness into your future. Because the next chapter of your life won't be written in struggle. It'll be written in quiet joy, honest connection, and deep, sustaining peace. You're not hard to love. You're just learning what true love finally feels like.

LEARNING LOVE LANGUAGES AND CHOOSING PEACE

Reclaiming the way you want to be loved.

Part 1: What I Was Taught Love Looked Like

Sometimes we learn love from broken places. From inconsistency. From survival. From giving too much and asking for too little.

Reflect on what love used to look like for you:

- I thought love meant always ________________________.
- I thought being chosen meant ______________________.
- I accepted _______________________ because I believed that was love.
- I confused attention with ___________________________.
- I gave too much of myself in order to ___________________.
- I stayed in situations where I felt _________________ because I feared being alone.
- I chased validation from people who ______________________.
- I thought love was earned by _______________________.
- I believed that suffering meant _________________________.
- I tolerated ____________________ to feel wanted.
- I lowered my standards in order to _____________________.

Now ask yourself: Was that really love, or was it attachment? Obligation? Familiarity?

Part 2: My True Love Language

The five classic love languages are:

- Words of affirmation
- Acts of service
- Physical touch
- Quality time
- Receiving gifts

Which one(s) resonate with you most right now?

____

My love language is: ______________________________________

How do you wish others would love you in this way?

____

____

How do you show this love to yourself?

____

____

Part 3: When Peace Becomes the Love Language

Eventually, we stop craving grand gestures and start craving something softer — something safer. We realize that peace is the highest form of love.

What does love rooted in peace look like to you now?

____

____

What do you no longer consider love?

____

____

Complete this declaration:

"I now choose love that feels like ____________ and no longer accept love that feels like ______________."

Peace is no longer optional — it's the standard. If it disturbs your spirit, it's not your home.

Sis.... Check In!

When was the last time you truly felt peaceful, and made it possible?

____

____

____

____

How does peace show up in your life? How can you invite more in?

____

____

____

____

What have you been tolerating that disrupts your peace? What would it look like to let that go?

____

____

____

____

How would your relationships change if you prioritized your peace over people-pleasing?

____

____

____

____

CHAPTER REFLECTION - HOW ARE YOU FEELING?

CONTINUE

I Am The Love I Was Looking For

I searched for what I already was — whole, worthy, and more than enough.

"Every time I begged to be chosen, I was abandoning myself. Now, I choose me — fully, finally, and without apology."

I used to look for love like it was a destination. Like if I found the right one – the one who called me beautiful, made me feel wanted, stayed through my storms – I would finally be okay. I'd be complete. I'd be safe. I'd be enough. So I gave too much. Settled too often. Waited too long. Every time I was left empty. I convinced myself that maybe if I just tried harder, loved deeper, gave more... they'd finally love me the way I loved them.

But the truth is, I was trying to get from others what I had never given to myself. I didn't know how to sit with myself. How to compliment myself. How to be proud of my reflection or trust my voice. I was loyal to people who weren't loyal to me, because I was still learning how to be loyal to myself. Then one day, I stopped running. I stopped begging. Stopped over-explaining my worth to people who were never meant to hold it.

I asked myself something I never had before: "What if the love you've been looking for... is already inside you?" That question changed everything. Because I realized that choosing myself isn't selfish – it's sacred. Speaking kindly to myself isn't vain – it's vital. Making myself the priority doesn't mean I love others less – it means I finally love me enough.

Now, I take myself on dates. I dance in the mirror. I affirm myself when doubt creeps in. I don't wait for someone to tell me I'm beautiful – I know I am. Because I've built a relationship with the most important person in my life.....ME. I used to think love had to come from someone else. But now I know... I am the love I was looking for all along.

Affirmation

"I don't need to be chosen — I choose me, completely."

Sis,

I know how much you've given. How often have you looked outside yourself for someone to call you worthy, beautiful, or enough? How many times have you settled, hoping that if you loved them right, they'd finally see you?

But I want you to pause right here. Say it with me: "I choose me." You don't need to be rescued. You don't need to be fixed. You are not missing anything. All the love you've been pouring into others? It's time to give that back to you. Speak life over your name. Take yourself out on dates. Spoil yourself. Praise yourself. Applaud your wins — even the small ones.

You are worthy of the love you've always dreamed about. Look at there, you've found it. She was here the whole time — in the mirror. But let's go deeper than that… Because loving yourself isn't just about bubble baths or affirmations. It's about how you speak to yourself when you mess up. It's about how you show up for yourself on the days when you don't feel beautiful or powerful or enough.

Self-love is discipline. It's grace. It's honesty. It's choosing not to abandon yourself again, even when you feel like running. So today, and every day after this one, make this promise to yourself: "I will love me… first. Fiercely. Fully. Forever." Because you are the love you've been waiting for this whole time. Hey girl hey.. It's so very nice to meet you. Now, let the rest of the world see you've arrived and you no longer need their validation.

FILL THIS HEART WITH YOU

A heart centered exercise to reclaim self-love.

You've spent so much of your life giving your love away — waiting for someone else to return it, prove it, hold it. But what if the love you were looking for... has always been you?

This page is your mirror. Inside the heart below, fill it with words, drawings, or phrases that reflect the love you now give to yourself.

You can write: Loving things you've discovered about yourself. Affirmations you want to believe. Memories where you showed up for you. What your self-love looks and feels like now.

Sis.... Check In!

In what ways have you looked for love outside of yourself?

How have you neglected your own needs while trying to be everything for someone else?

What does it mean to love yourself fully, without waiting for someone else to do it first?

How can you deepen your relationship with yourself starting today?

CHAPTER REFLECTION - HOW ARE YOU FEELING?

CONTINUE

Unapologetically HER

She stopped editing her essence to make other people comfortable.

"I am no longer who I had to become to survive. I am who I was always meant to be — free, whole, and finally… me."

For a long time, I made myself small. I bit my tongue. Dimmed my light. Smiled politely in rooms where I wanted to scream. Let's face it, some people will test your gangster like none other. I showed up how I thought they needed me to – Polished. Palatable. Predictable.

I watered down my truth so I wouldn't seem "too much," and I lost myself trying to make everyone else comfortable. But not anymore. There came a day when I looked in the mirror and said: "I'm tired of apologizing for existing." Tired of saying sorry for outgrowing people who were never growing with me. Tired of downplaying my accomplishments so I wouldn't seem intimidating. Tired of hiding my pain, my power, my presence. Because here's what I know now: I was never "too much." They were just not enough to handle the magnitude of a woman rising in her truth.

I don't owe anyone an explanation for my boundaries, my glow-up, my healing, or my joy. I don't need to shrink so someone else can feel tall. I don't need to dim my brilliance to make someone else feel brave. I am finally, fully, unapologetically me. The woman I've become is honest. She's powerful. She's soft. She's wise. She's whole. She's not explaining her evolution to anybody. Let them adjust. Let them whisper. Let them call it ego if they want to. Because I know the truth: this isn't ego – it's arrival.

What they're really witnessing... is freedom. It took me years to unlearn the habit of shrinking. Now that I've expanded, I'm not folding myself back up to fit inside their expectations. This isn't arrogance – it's awareness.

I finally know who I am. I'm not about to apologize for arriving. You don't have to like her. But you will respect her. Because she's not backing down, playing small, or biting her tongue anymore. She's here. She's loud with her healing. She's glowing without permission. Guess what? She's never going back.

Affirmation

I don't shrink, I expandd—unapologetically, boldly, and beautifully.

Sis,

You've spent enough time asking for permission to be you. Enough time explaining your worth, proving your heart, shrinking your shine. But that season is over now.

This is the part where you walk into the room and own it. Where you laugh with your full chest. Where you speak your mind — even if your voice shakes. Where you wear the red lipstick, post the picture, take up the space.

You don't owe this world a watered-down version of yourself. You don't have to make your light more "digestible." You are not intimidating — they just weren't prepared for a woman who knows who she is. Make a declaration to your younger self that she needed to hear. Go over the things that have held you back up until this point. Speak the truth you've been softening for far too long. If they call it too loud, too bold, too much, good. That means you're finally being real. Your finally being honest. Finally owning your shit. You go girl.

THE UNAPOLOGETIC AFFIRMATION WALL

Write "I am" statements on virtual bricks below — building a wall of self-trust and confidence. Examples: I am powerful even when I'm still. I am allowed to take up space.

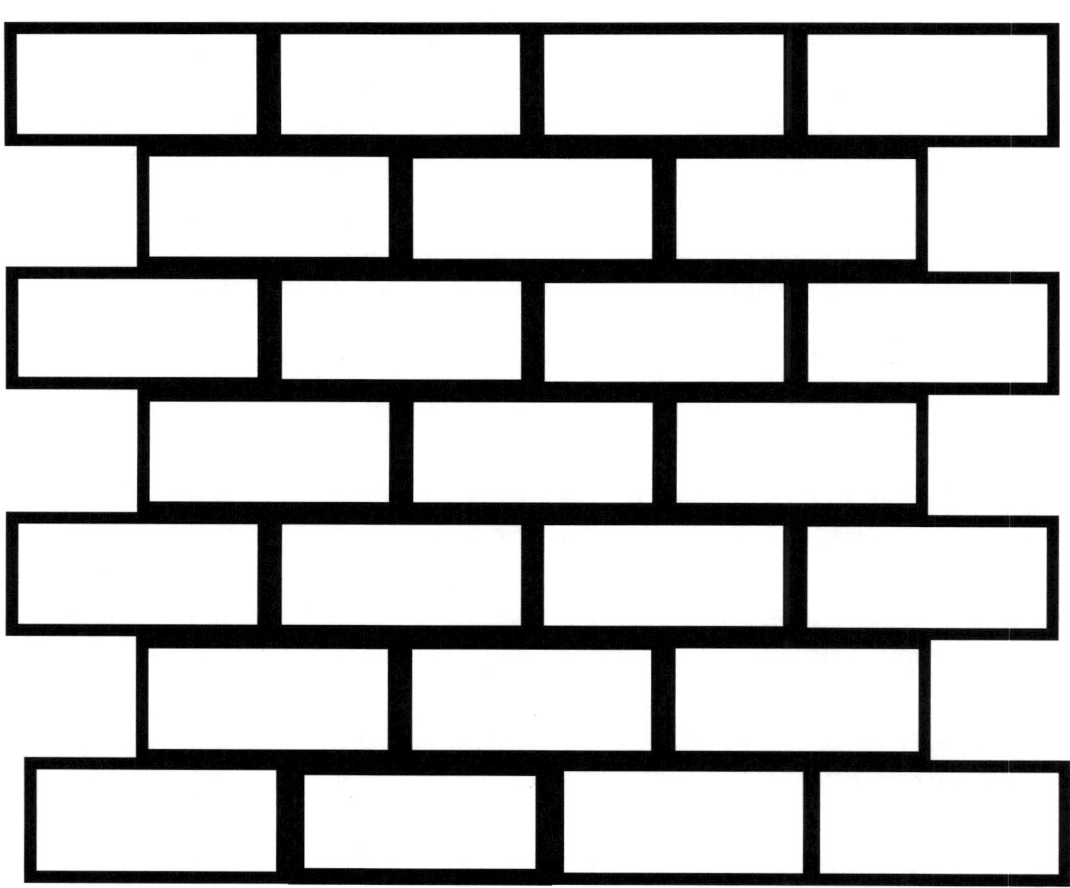

VISION BOARD

A Creative Snapshot of the Woman You're Becoming

This vision board allows you to draw, write, paste photos, or fill it in with phrases that align with the version of HER that's rising in you.

Sis.... Check In!

In what ways have you dimmed your light to make others more comfortable?

What parts of you did you silence, soften, or suppress just be accepted?

What does it mean for you to live as your full self - unapologetically?

How does it feel to walk away from spaces that only want your presence, not your well-being?

CHAPTER REFLECTION - HOW ARE YOU FEELING?

CONTINUE

My Softness Is "SACRED"

Being soft in a hard world is not weakness. It's divine.

"I used to wear hardness like a shield. But my softness? That's where my soul lives."

For a long time, I believed that being soft meant being weak. That if I let my guard down, if I cried too often, if I loved too deeply — I'd be taken advantage of. Again. So I became hard. Sharp with my tongue. Guarded with my heart. Selective with my energy.

Honestly, that version of me was necessary for a season. She was surviving. She kept me safe. But she was also tired. Because the truth is... I'm not built to be cold. I'm not built to live in defense mode. I'm not built to flinch every time someone gets too close. My softness is not a liability. It's a gift.

The world taught me to armor up. But healing taught me that my softness is where my power lives. The way I care. The way I nurture. The way I feel deeply and love hard. That is sacred. That is divine. That is me. I've learned that I don't have to be strong every day. I don't have to carry everyone's weight. I don't have to prove my toughness to be respected.

Now, I honor the tears. I honor the stillness. I honor the gentle spirit in me that just wants to breathe. Soft doesn't mean broken. Soft means I've survived the worst of life and still choose to keep my heart open. I don't need to harden myself to earn safety. I am safe — within me. Any space, person, or relationship that doesn't honor my softness... doesn't deserve my presence. Because my softness is earned. It's seasoned. It's sacred. It came from walking through hell and still choosing to feel. Still choosing to love. Still choosing to be me. I'm no longer ashamed of the woman who tears up during a commercial, who overthinks, who loves out loud, who needs quiet, who craves comfort, who holds people a little tighter. That softness is where the real strength is. Now that I've found her again — I'm never letting her go.

Affirmation

"My softness is not weakness — it's wisdom, it's healing, it's holy."

Sis,

You don't have to be strong every day. You don't have to be the rock, the fixer, the "I got it" woman all the time. You are allowed to rest. To cry. To feel. This is your permission slip to stop holding your breath. You've been wearing armor for so long — maybe now it's time to slip into something softer.

Let yourself be held. By safe people. By stillness. By your arms. Let your heart come down from high alert. Let the version of you that's always been soft and tender and loving come back home. Softness doesn't mean broken — it means you still believe in love. Get back in tune with who she is. Invite her back in. Remind her she's not a problem to be solved. She is sacred. She is strong. She is welcome here. Let her take up space again. Let her speak without apology. Let her feel safe in her sensitivity, knowing that the world doesn't get to define what strength looks like anymore.

Because being soft after everything you've survived is not weakness — that's bravery with a heartbeat. So exhale, baby girl. Take off the armor. Wrap yourself in grace. You made it. Now, you get to rest.

Welcome home.

SOFTNESS INVENTORY

Rediscover the power of your tenderness.

Complete the following:

- My softness is not weakness, it is ____________________
- I used to hide my softness because ____________________
- I now protect my softness by ____________________
- When I allow myself to be soft, I feel ____________________
- My softness helps others by ____________________
- The world taught me to harden when ____________________
- I reclaim my softness by ____________________
- My softness is a gift that allows me to ____________________
- I used to confuse softness with ____________________
- I feel powerful in my softness when ____________________
- My softness protects me from ____________________
- One way I soften with intention is ____________________
- I admire softness in others because ____________________
- Softness taught me that I don't need to ____________________
- When I soften, I reconnect with ____________________
- I no longer shrink my softness for ____________________
- The softness I miss most in myself is ____________________
- I invite softness into my day by ____________________
- The bravest thing I've done softly is ____________________
- My softness is a gift that allows me to ____________________
- I used to confuse softness with ____________________
- I feel powerful in my softness when ____________________
- My softness protects me from ____________________
- One way I soften with intention is ____________________
- I admire softness in others because ____________________
- Softness taught me that I don't need to ____________________
- When I soften, I reconnect with ____________________
- I no longer shrink my softness for ____________________
- The softness I miss most in myself is ____________________
- I invite softness into my day by ____________________
- The bravest thing I've done softly is ____________________

"I don't need to toughen up to be worthy. I only need to remember: my softness is sacred."

THE SOFT PROMISE CARD

A sacred contract between you and your healing self

Instructions: In the box below, write a short promise to honor your softness, no matter what the world says. Speak gently. This is your love note to you.

Example: "I will no longer apologize for needing rest, stillness, or space to feel. I am not hard to love. I am already enough. I will protect my softness like sacred ground."

"My Soft Promise"

Now sign and date it below:

Signature: ____________________ ***Date:*** ____________

Let this promise be your permission slip to live unguarded, unhurried, and unapologetically soft.

MY
SOFTNESS
IS SACRED

Sis.... Check In!

When did you first learn to associate softness with weakness?

In what ways have you hidden or suppressed your tender side to survive?

What does being soft look like for you now in your healing era?

What would it feel like to fully embrace your femininity, your sensitivity, your soul?

CHAPTER REFLECTION - HOW ARE YOU FEELING?

CONTINUE

Chapter 19

She's Not The One You Used To Know

The healed version of her walks different — because she carries nothing she didn't choose.

"They don't recognize you because they only remember who you were when you didn't know who you were."

Let them talk. Let them whisper. Let them tell the old stories about the version of you they used to know. Because they don't know this one. They don't know the woman who had to break to be rebuilt. The one who had to lose herself to find her again. The one who had to cry in silence, rise in private, and come back with fire in her chest.

I have sheltered myself from the world so much because I was afraid of getting hurt. I made myself small — quieter, softer, easier — all to keep the peace. I didn't want to ruffle feathers. I didn't want to be called too much. So I stayed in places that drained me just to avoid confrontation. Now I've become a bit of a savage. I'll tell you how I feel. I'll give you honesty. But you only get so many chances with me. There's only so many times you can let people play in your face before you look in the mirror and say, "If this is who you are, then let me show you who I can be."

Not out of malice, but because I know my worth now, and I protect it at all costs. I give myself five minutes to cry, scream, vent — whatever I need. Then I keep going. This new version of me doesn't dwell. She decides. I no longer live for words. If your actions don't match what you say, you can stay the hell away from me.

I'm not the one you used to know. That version of me tolerated too much. She over-gave. She second-guessed. She made excuses for people who never showed up. But she's not here anymore. This version of me is clear, grounded and very unshakable.

She's not going to beg to be seen — she walks in the room and takes up space. If that makes people uncomfortable, they were never meant to be around for this version anyway.

Affirmation

"I no longer shrink to fit into rooms I've outgrown. If they don't recognize me, that's fine — I've evolved."

Sis,

It's okay if they don't recognize you anymore. You're not her anymore. Not the one who tolerated the bare minimum. Not the one who explained her heart to people who never deserved the access. Not the one who begged to be seen. You've evolved. You've softened and strengthened at the same time. You've learned that becoming her meant shedding everything that dimmed you.

Guess what? You don't owe anybody a memo. You don't have to prove your growth. You just have to own it. So take this page and declare it: "I'm not the one you used to know. I'm better." If they want access to this new version of you? They'll have to rise to your level now. Because you're not lowering your standards just to make someone feel comfortable. You're not backtracking on your healing to make others feel less convicted. You're not apologizing for becoming exactly who you were always meant to be.

Let them watch. Let them whisper. Let them wonder how you did it. Because while they were busy trying to keep you in your past — you were busy becoming unforgettable.

LET ME REINTRODUCE MYSELF

A bold letter to reclaim your identity and express who you are now.

Let me reintroduce myself — not to impress you, not to convince you, but to honor the woman I've fought to become. I am no longer the girl who ________________, the one who kept quiet to avoid conflict, who gave without boundaries, and apologized for shining too brightly. I've grown into someone who ______________, someone who walks with intention and leads with purpose. I value ______________ over ______________ now, and I've stopped trading my peace for approval.
I walk into rooms with ______________, not seeking to be chosen but knowing I already am. I speak like someone who knows ______________, not because I need to be loud, but because I refuse to stay silent. I no longer explain ______________, and I've made peace with ______________.
I protect my energy by ______________, even when it disappoints others. The version of me you once knew couldn't ______________, but this version of me will never ______________ again. I don't need you to understand this evolution — I just need you to respect it.

You may remember who I was, but this is who I am now: a woman who knows herself deeply, loves herself fiercely, and chooses herself without apology.

Signed,

The evolved version of me.

THE ALLIGNMENT COMPASS

A self-guided map to help you stay grounded in your evolved truth.

Use this compass to navigate who you are now, what you stand for, and where you're going. Let this be your internal guide when the world tries to make you forget.

My North Star (Purpose) ______________________________

My Core Energy ___________________________

What I No Longer Allow ___________________________

What Keeps Me Aligned ___________________________

The Boundaries I Honor ___________________________

How I Return to Myself ___________________________

What I Trust in This Season ___________________________

"When the noise gets loud, I come home to this compass. It always points back to ME."

MY 5 CORE VALUES

A clarity tool for knowing who you are and what you stand on.

Instructions: In the space below, list the five values that matter most to you — the ones you use to guide your choices, relationships, boundaries, and future.

Core 1. ______________________________________

Core 2. ______________________________________

Core 3. ______________________________________

Core 4. ______________________________________

Core 5. ______________________________________

Now reflect:

- Which value do I live out loud the most? ____________________
- Which one do I need to honor more? ______________________

"When a woman knows what she stands for, no one can shake her foundation."

Sis.... Check In!

What version of yourself have you finally outgrown - and why?

Who still tries to relate to the older version of you, and how does that make you feel?

What does this new version of you know that the old you didn't?

How are you showing up differently now - in love, in boundaries, in your presence?

CHAPTER REFLECTION - HOW ARE YOU FEELING?

CONTINUE

She's Gone And I Don't Miss Her

The funeral wasn't sad. It was sacred.

"I didn't lose her. I laid her to rest — with honor, with truth, and with love. She wasn't built to carry the woman I was becoming."

There are no flowers. No black dress. No sad songs playing in the background. This is a celebration of life. This is a release. Because the woman I used to be... She's gone, and I don't miss her. I don't miss the way she begged for love. I don't miss the way she poured from an empty cup. I don't miss how she made herself small just to be chosen.

I don't miss the way she smiled through pain, hoping someone... anyone... would finally notice she was drowning. I hated how she let people walk over her. I hated how she gave second, third, and tenth chances to people who were never worthy of the first. I hated how she trusted everyone but herself. I hated how she chose others before she even thought about choosing herself. I hated how invisible she felt. How replaceable. How easily discarded she was by people who only came around when they needed something. I hated that she never knew she was allowed to put herself first. That she thought being good meant being silent. That she mistook survival for love.

But you know what else? I honor her because even though she was broken, she still showed up. Even though she was tired, she still kept going. Even though she was scared, she still dreamed of more. That is why I can finally bury her—not with shame, not with regret — But with gratitude. I bury her with grace, with wisdom, with clarity, with love. She served her purpose. She was the foundation for the woman I am now — Unapologetic. Boundaries. Loved. Whole. She's gone, and I don't miss her. Not even a little. Because I am finally here. Fully. Boldly. Unmistakably me.

This time, I'm not asking for permission. I'm not waiting to be chosen. I'm not hoping to be understood. I am choosing me — out loud, on purpose, and without apology. The door is closed. That chapter is over. The girl who needed saving is no longer running the show. I didn't lose her — I outgrew her. Now that she's gone, I finally have room to breathe. To become. To rise. So no, I don't miss her. Not her pain. Not her fear. Not her silence. Not her tolerance. Not her tears. I thank her for surviving — But I live for the woman who's finally thriving. I buried her with beauty and grace. But I walked away with Wisdom, Freedom, Acceptance, and Peace. Let me finally re-introduce myself... Hey everyone, I'm Le' Shawnda, and I am in love with this new version of me. I'm finally living. I'm finally free.

Affirmation

I honor the woman I was…but I don't mourn her. I've evolved, and I'm not looking back.

Sis,

I want to thank you — and let you go. Thank you for holding it together when everything around you was falling apart. Thank you for showing up when you were exhausted, for smiling when your heart was breaking, for keeping the lights on in your soul when everything felt dark.

I want you to thank yourself for loving even when you weren't loved back. For forgiving when it wasn't asked for. For standing in rooms where you were never truly seen. Thank you for carrying burdens that were never meant for you. Say to yourself; I send you love — without judgment, and I say goodbye. Because now, I'm finally living.

Not just existing. Not just surviving. Living. Laughing. Loving. Becoming. And I deserve this version of me. She's bold. She's healed. She's grounded in her worth and glowing in her truth. She's the woman you used to dream about. She's everything you weren't sure you could become. And she's not going anywhere. So rest now. You don't have to fight anymore. You got us this far. I'll take it from here.

YOU BURIED HER NOW LET HER GO

You let her go. You named the pain. You stopped romanticizing survival. That is a sacred act. Now, we mark that shift with a creative release that helps you process it physically and spiritually.

Part 1: Her Final Words

Imagine you are writing from the perspective of your old self — the one you just buried. What would she say in her final goodbye? Let her speak one last time. No bitterness. Just truth.

Write her final message here:

____

____

____

____

____

____

____

____

____

____

____

____

____

____

____

Part 2: Your Eulogy to Her

What did she teach you? What are you grateful for, even in the hurt?
Write your farewell speech to the woman you used to be. Keep it honest. Keep it loving.

Part 3: What Rises in Her Place

In the space below, write 10 things you are ready to become now that she is no longer running the show.

1 ____

2 ____

3 ____

4 ____

5 ____

6 ____

7 ____

8 ____

9 ____

10 ____

Sis.... Check In!

What parts of your past self have you finally outgrown?

What are you releasing her from - spiritually, mentally, emotionally?

What would you say at her goodbye - not in grief, but in gratitude?

What do you love most about this new version of you?

CHAPTER REFLECTION - HOW ARE YOU FEELING?

CONTINUE

30 DAYS TO BURY HER AND BECOME YOU

1	***Call Her Out*** **Soul Prompt:** Who is the version of you that you're burying? Describe her without shame. **Action Step:** Write her a goodbye letter — uncensored. **Affirmation:** "I no longer live in survival mode. I choose to be free."
2	***The Mirror Doesn't Lie*** **Soul Prompt:** What do you see when you look at yourself — and what do you want to see? **Action Step:** Stand in front of the mirror and speak 3 loving truths out loud. **Affirmation:** "I am not my mistakes. I am my becoming."
3	***Say Her Name*** **Soul Prompt:** Name the patterns, people, or pain you're ready to release. **Action Step:** Speak them aloud, then say: "I release you." **Affirmation:** "I release what I cannot carry into my next level."
4	***Write the Eulogy*** **Soul Prompt:** Write a one-paragraph eulogy for the version of you you're letting go of. **Action Step:** Light a candle and read it aloud. **Affirmation:** "I honor who I was, but I no longer live there."
5	***Burn the Rules*** **Soul Prompt:** What rules were you taught about womanhood that no longer serve you? **Action Step:** Rip them up (literally or symbolically). **Affirmation:** "I don't shrink to be loved. I expand to be seen."
6	***Breathe Again*** **Soul Prompt:** What does peace feel like in your body? **Action Step:** Try a 4-4-4 breath: Inhale 4, hold 4, exhale 4. Repeat. **Affirmation:** "My breath is a sacred reset."
7	***Reintroduce Yourself*** **Soul Prompt:** Who are you becoming? Describe her in vivid detail. **Action Step:** Say her name in the mirror. **Affirmation:** "I am no longer hidden. I am here."

30 DAYS TO BURY HER AND BECOME YOU

8	***Forgive Her*** **Soul Prompt:** What's the one thing you've struggled to forgive yourself for? **Action Step:** Write it down, say "I forgive you," then tear or fold it away. **Affirmation:** "Forgiveness is freedom, and I choose both."
9	***Detox Your Yes*** **Soul Prompt:** Where have you said "yes" when you really meant "no"? **Action Step:** Write a list of boundaries you will start enforcing. **Affirmation:** "No is a full sentence."
10	***Say No More*** **Soul Prompt:** What cycle are you finally ready to end? **Action Step:** Draw a line in your journal. On one side: the old. On the other: the new. Affirmation: "This ends with me."
11	***Clean the Closet*** **Soul Prompt:** What are you holding onto that no longer fits your spirit? **Action Step:** Donate or throw out one physical item that carries old energy. **Affirmation:** "I release what no longer aligns."
12	***Touch Yourself With Grace*** **Soul Prompt:** What has your body been through that you never thanked it for? **Action Step:** Gently rub lotion or oil on your skin with intention and love. **Affirmation:** "My body is not broken. It is a blessing."
13	***Talk to God*** **Soul Prompt:** What do you need to release in prayer or surrender? **Action Step:** Write a letter to God or speak aloud what you've been holding in. **Affirmation:** "I don't have to carry it all. I can lay it down."
14	***Laugh Again*** **Soul Prompt:** When was the last time you belly-laughed? What brings you joy? **Action Step:** Watch, listen to, or do something that makes you laugh. **Affirmation:** "Joy belongs to me, too."

30 DAYS TO BURY HER AND BECOME YOU

15	***Permission to Rest*** **Soul Prompt:** Where in your life are you tired of performing strength? **Action Step:** Take a nap. Say no. Rest. **Affirmation:** "Rest is my right, not my reward."
16	***Mirror the Queen*** **Soul Prompt:** What makes you beautiful beyond appearance? **Action Step:** Write it in lipstick or post-it on your mirror. **Affirmation:** "I am beauty, embodied and whole."
17	***Reclaim the Room*** **Soul Prompt:** What parts of yourself have you abandoned to be accepted? **Action Step:** Take up space today. Speak boldly. Take your time. **Affirmation:** "I will not shrink to fit into small places."
18	***Sit With the Silence*** **Soul Prompt:** What are you afraid to hear when the world gets quiet? **Action Step:** Sit in silence for 10 minutes. Let it speak. **Affirmation:** "Stillness makes room for my truth."
19	***Protect Your Peace*** **Soul Prompt:** Who or what is currently disturbing your peace? **Action Step:** Create a "peace plan" to manage or release it. **Affirmation:** "My peace is not up for negotiation."
20	***Say It Like You Mean It*** **Soul Prompt:** What truth are you scared to say out loud? **Action Step:** Whisper it. Speak it. Shout it. Claim it. **Affirmation:** "My voice is not a threat. It's a gift."
21	***Soft Is Still Strong*** **Soul Prompt:** Where have you confused hardness with protection? **Action Step:** Do one thing today that makes you feel soft, safe, and whole. **Affirmation:** "My softness is sacred."

30 DAYS TO BURY HER AND BECOME YOU

22	***Update the Story*** **Soul Prompt:** What narrative have you outgrown? What's the new one? **Action Step:** Write 3 sentences that reflect who you are now. **Affirmation:** "I am the author of my next chapter."
23	***Choose Her Daily*** **Soul Prompt:** What does it look like to choose yourself on a Tuesday, not just when it's hard? **Action Step:** Do one small thing for you today. **Affirmation:** "I choose myself without guilt."
24	***Light a Candle*** **Soul Prompt:** What needs a symbolic release in your life? **Action Step:** Light a candle and let it burn with intention. **Affirmation:** "I let go and light the way forward."
25	***Celebrate the Shift*** **Soul Prompt:** What do you love about this version of you? **Action Step:** Celebrate her. Toast her. Post about her. Dance with her. **Affirmation:** "I am proud of the woman I'm becoming."
26	***Let Love In*** **Soul Prompt:** What have you pushed away out of fear or habit? **Action Step:** Practice receiving today: a compliment, help, a kind word. **Affirmation:** "I am worthy of love in all its forms."
27	***Walk Like Her*** **Soul Prompt:** How does the healed version of you move through the world? **Action Step:** Walk, talk, dress, or carry yourself as her today. **Affirmation:** "I am already who I'm becoming."
28	***Be Witnessed*** **Soul Prompt:** What have you carried in silence? Who do you trust to hold your truth? **Action Step:** Share a part of your story with someone safe. **Affirmation:** "My story is sacred. My voice is valid."

30 DAYS TO BURY HER AND BECOME YOU

29	***Write Her a Love Letter*** **Soul Prompt:** Write a letter to the version of you who made it through. **Action Step:** Seal it. Keep it. Reread it often. **Affirmation:** "I love the woman I fought to become."
30	***Bury Her With Grace*** **Soul Prompt:** What are you finally ready to bury for good? **Action Step:** Light a candle. Burn a page. Say a prayer. Bury it. Let it be. **Affirmation:** "She's gone. And I don't miss her."

Your 30-day challenge now closes with a soft, empowering final note — a reminder that her healing is just beginning. This journey wasn't about fixing yourself — it was about finding yourself. You've done something courageous. You showed up. You released. You remembered your power. Let this be your new foundation — not a finish line. You are sacred. You are whole. And you are just getting started.

Even on the days you feel unsure, unworthy, or undone — come back to this. Come back to you. You are never too far gone to begin again. You are proof that healing doesn't have to be loud — it just has to be true. I hope you revisit these pages often. Let them hold you. Let them remind you. Because you, beloved — you are the evidence of resurrection. And the world is better with the healed version of you in it.

With deep love and light,

Le' Shawnda Riley-Lovelace

Congratulations

Look at you. You showed up for your healing — even when it hurt. Even when it was heavy. Even when life tried to convince you to stay silent, small, or stuck. But you didn't. You chose truth. You chose release. You chose you.

Maybe you cried. Maybe you screamed. Maybe you took breaks between pages because it got too real. That's okay. That means it worked. That means you worked.

You made it to the end of this book — but more importantly, you made it to the beginning of a new version of yourself. One that no longer needs to be explained. One that is whole, sacred, bold, and packed with beautiful boundaries.

So this is your moment. Celebrate it. Stand in front of the mirror and meet the woman who didn't just read through these pages — she transformed through them. You buried her. You grieved her. You released her with grace.

Welcome to your becoming. You are HER now.

With deep love and unwavering pride,

—The Woman You Fought to Become

JOIN THE TRIBE

Join Us on Facebook

Healing doesn't end on the last page — and you don't have to keep growing alone. Join our private Facebook group, a sacred space created just for women like you.

This is a judgment-free zone, where we cry, celebrate, share, and rise together. Whether you're still in the middle of your journey or finally breathing in your breakthrough, this is a space where your story matters.

Come talk about the book, your experiences, your healing, and your truth — surrounded by women who get it.

You are not alone. We journey together.

Search: She's Not Coming Back — The Healing Circle on Facebook and request to join. We can't wait to meet you there.

Check Out Our Playlist On Spotify

About ME

Le' Shawnda Riley-Lovelace is a woman of strength, survival, and sacred evolution. A mother, wife, sister, daughter, friend, and entrepreneur — she is living proof that even after seasons of silence, self-sacrifice, and soul-wrenching trials, it's still possible to rise. She is unshakable. Unmovable. And most importantly, she is real — a reflection of every woman who's ever questioned her worth and is now reclaiming it, one boundary and one breath at a time.

This book was written as an ode to the woman she used to be — the version she buried with grace as she prepares to step fully into her next chapter. As she approaches 50, Le' Shawnda bares her soul not for applause, but for freedom. Her deepest hope is that these pages become a mirror for every reader: a space to feel, to release, to remember who she is, and to know — without apology — that she is sacred, worthy, and allowed to take up space. Always.

Made in the USA
Columbia, SC
21 June 2025